HOW CAN I EXPERIMENT WITH ... ?

SOUND

Cindy Devine Dalton

Cindy Devine Dalton graduated from Ball State University, Indiana,
with a Bachelor of Science degree in Health Science.
For several years she taught medical science in grades 9-12.

Teresa and Ed Sikora

Teresa Sikora teaches 4th grade math and science. She graduated with a
Bachelor of Science in Elementary Education and recently attained National Certification
for Middle Childhood Generalist. She is married with two children.
Ed Sikora is an Aerospace Engineer, working on the Space Shuttle Main Engines.
He earned a Bachelors of Science degree in Aerospace Engineering from the
University of Florida and a Masters Degree in Computer Science from the
Florida Institute of Technology.

Rourke Publishing LLC
Vero Beach, Florida 32964

PROJECT EDITORS
Teresa and Ed Sikora

PHOTO CREDITS
Corel
Gibbons Photography
Walt Burkett, Photographer

ILLUSTRATIONS
Kathleen Carreiro

EDITORIAL SERVICES
Pamela Schroeder

Library of Congress Cataloging-in-Publication Data

Dalton, Cindy Devine, 1964–
    Sound / Cindy Devine Dalton.
        p. cm. — (How can I experiment with?)
    Includes bibliographical references and index
    ISBN 1-58952-015-7
    1. Sound—Juvenile literature. 2. Sound—Experiments—Juvenile literature. [1. Sound. 2. Sound—
Experiments 3.Experiments.] I.Title

QC225.5 D35 2001
534.078—dc21   00-067072

Printed in the USA

Sound: A vibration that travels through a substance, such as air, and can be heard.

Quote:

"Music is the arithmetic of sounds…"

-Claude Debussy

Table of Contents

If There Were No Ears

Do you think about sound? What do you think sound is made of? Would there be sound if there were no ears to hear it? Can you feel sound? Learning about sound will be an "ear" opening experience. So hold on to your ears and "feel" the next sound.

We can hear and feel sound. Our ears turn the vibrations into sound, but our bodies can feel it too. Place your fingers on your throat and sing.

Sound Is a Vibration

Sound is sometimes terrible. It is also beautiful. It can be loud, quiet, soft, or harsh. How does it get that way? If you are in a room with loud music, you can feel the vibrations in the air. You can also feel the vibrations in the floor, walls, and furniture. That's what sound is—vibrations in the air, wood, metal, water, or any medium.

Tunnels can make sounds seem louder.

What Do Ears Do?

Your ear has three parts—the outer ear, middle ear, and the inner ear. The middle ear contains fluid and tiny hairs. Sound vibrations move through the fluid. The fluid moves the tiny hairs that send electrical impulses to the brain. The brain takes the impulses and turns them into sounds we can understand.

Vibrations in the air cause the fluid in the middle ear to move. That sends impulses to the brain, and the brain turns them into sound.

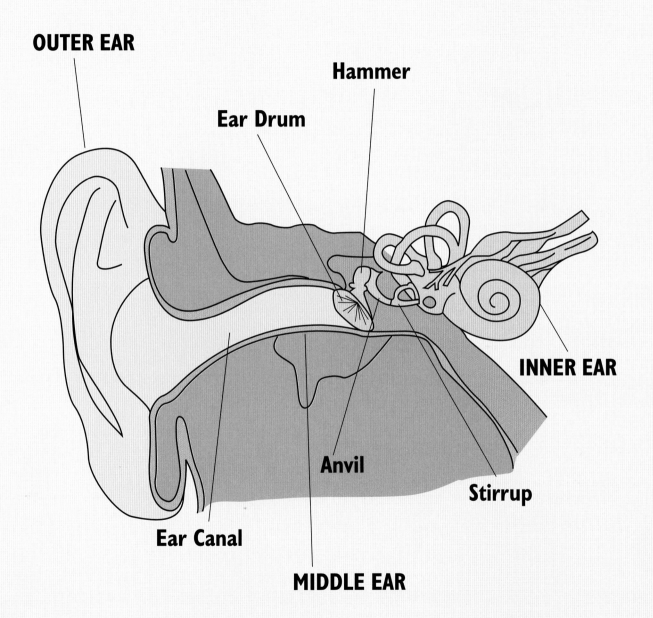

OUTER EAR

Ear Drum

Hammer

INNER EAR

Anvil

Ear Canal

Stirrup

MIDDLE EAR

Is Sound Everywhere?

Sound is everywhere except one place. There can be no sound in a **vacuum**. Outer space is a vacuum. Sounds need something to travel through. Sound not only travels through air but through all kinds of things! Try this the next time you're in a pool: have a friend talk to you underwater while you listen. It may be hard to understand what your friend is saying, but you're really hearing sound waves travel through water. Actually, sound waves travel faster through the water than through the air. This is an example of sound moving through a medium. That's why there is no sound in space because there is nothing to travel through.

Sound travels faster through water than air.

No Sound in a Vacuum?

If there is no sound in space, how can the astronauts talk with us here on Earth? This is a tricky one! The sounds astronauts hear are sound waves that have been changed into **electromagnetic** waves and back again. Electromagnetic waves, like radio waves, can travel through a vacuum like space. Then they are turned back into sound waves. Imagine radio waves traveling to your radio. They are traveling through the air, but you can't hear them. When you turn on your radio, they are changed back into sound waves! Cool huh? The same thing happens when these waves travel through space to reach the astronauts.

The portable phone in your home, your radio, and even walkie-talkies pick up and convert sound waves.

What Makes Sound Sound Different?

Different vibrations make different kinds of sounds. Imagine a tight string being plucked, moving up and down. A cycle of a string moving up and down is called a vibration. The faster the string moves up and down, the faster the vibration is. The rate of the vibration is called the **frequency**.
An example of this can be seen by looking at a guitar. When you see a thin string pulled tight and plucked, you hear a high sound. When you see a thick string being plucked, it moves slower. It makes a low sound. A fast vibration makes a high **pitch**. A slow vibration makes a low pitch.

Pluck the strings on a guitar and listen to the different sounds each string makes.

17

What Frequency Sounds Good?

Frequency can be very slow or very fast. We choose the sounds we like by their **tone**. A tone is a sound that repeats its frequency, or has only small changes in the frequency. For example, most of the songs you sing have about the same tone all the way through. Sounds that have changing tones or frequencies can sound bad to us. Is there a type of music that you don't like? Is it because of the tone, or the words?

Beating on drums can sound bad. However, drums can sound good when they are played in a tone.

Hands on:

Make a Flute

What you need:

- A straw
- Scissors
- Someone who can blow really hard

Try This:

1. Use the scissors to cut off the tip of the straw to a point. (Try to get both sides to be the same!)
2. Gently chew on the pointed tips. Try to soften the edges and push the tips together. The two tips should almost touch each other.
3. Ask the person who can blow really hard to put the pointy end in his or her mouth, and blow really hard. If you do it right (it might take some practice), you will get a very loud sound from the flute.

Try This, Too:

1. Cut off the non-pointy end of the straw. What does this do to the tone?
2. Can you cut holes in the straw so that you can play it like a real flute?
3. Slide a second straw over the first. You can make a straw trombone!

What Happened?

When you blow on the end of the straw, the two pieces of the tip vibrate together and that makes sound. The vibration travels down the straw and bounces back from the end. This causes a wave in the air inside the straw. The wave bounces back and forth between the two ends. This is the vibration that you are hearing!

Changing the length of the straw (by clipping it off, or by making a straw trombone) makes a different pitch. It changes the time it takes for the vibration to travel up and down the straw. Making a hole in the straw, so it is like a real flute, lets the vibration bounce back from where the hole is. That also changes the pitch.

The Sounds of Music

Instruments are made with different matcrials. There are strings, wood, leather, and metals. Brass instruments cause faster vibrations, giving louder sounds. How do you think instruments made of wood would sound?

There are many instruments that you can make at home. All you need to do is gather up spoons, cans, strings, and beans to make all kinds of sounds. Get your friends together and have your own band. Making music can be lots of fun.

This tiny violin will make a higher pitched sound than a full-size one.

Sound off:

Silly Sound Questions

Question:

Why do whales sing?

Answer:

Whales sing for several different reasons. They sing to mark their territories in the ocean and to talk to other whales. They sing in different ways. Some whales sing by making chirping noises, clicking their jaws together, moaning, or whistling. Whales sing the same "tune" in the same seasons. When the seasons change, so do their tunes. It may be like the songs we sing during different holidays.

Whales talk to each other underwater using sound waves. These waves can sometimes travel for miles.

Question:

Why do cats purr?

Answer:

Cats do not make themselves purr. They do not realize they are purring, like we are not aware of our breathing. It just happens. They purr when they are happy, content, and sometimes afraid. A purring cat is not a threat. Sometimes cats purr to other cats to signal peace.

28

The purring sound we hear is the vibrations of air in the cat's **diaphragm**. The diaphragm is below the chest and above the stomach.

Question:
Why does it hurt my ears when someone scratches their fingernails on a chalkboard?

Answer:
Some materials make vibrations that sound very nice. Other materials don't. Fingernails scraping a chalkboard make a lot of vibrations quickly. The chalkboard can't absorb the vibrations. Quick vibrations make a sound that is high pitched and loud.

29

Glossary

diaphragm (DY eh fram) — the part of your body that helps you breathe by pushing and pulling your lungs

frequency (FREE kwen see) — how quickly something happens over and over again

electromagnetic (ih lek troh mag NET ik)— a wave that moves through space, made of magnetic and electric fields

medium (MEE dee em) — any substance or material through which something (like sound waves) can move

pitch (PICH) — how high or low a sound is

tone (TOHN) — a musical note, the sound of one note

vacuum (VAK you em) — space that has no matter in it

Further Reading

Let's Wonder About Science, Rourke Press, 1995
Energy And Action, Rourke Press, 1995

Websites to visit

www.enchantedlearning.com
www.fatlion.com
www.smarterkids.com

Index